# TARANTULAS

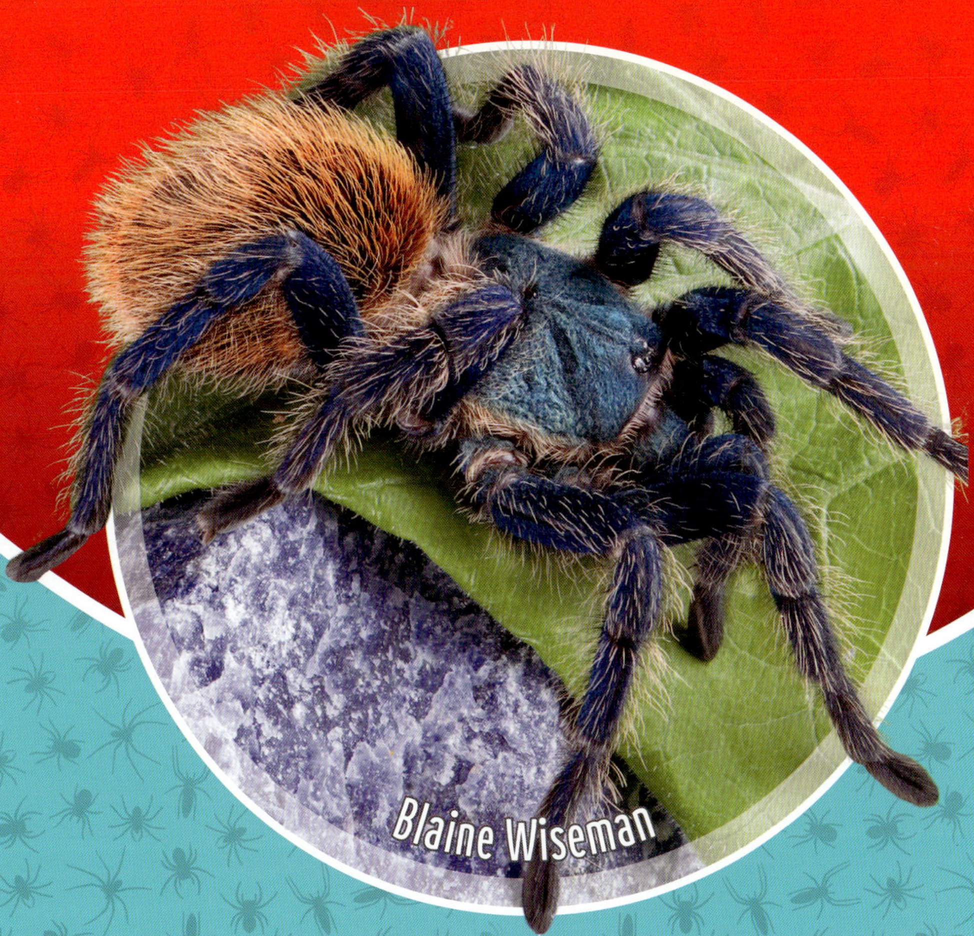

Blaine Wiseman

SPIDERS

www.av2books.com

### Step 1
Go to www.av2books.com

### Step 2
Enter this unique code

**IUDTHZN4H**

### Step 3
Explore your interactive eBook!

AV2 is optimized for use on any device

# Your interactive eBook comes with...

**Contents**
Browse a live contents page to easily navigate through resources

**Audio**
Listen to sections of the book read aloud

**Videos**
Watch informative video clips

**Weblinks**
Gain additional information for research

**Try This!**
Complete activities and hands-on experiments

**Key Words**
Study vocabulary, and complete a matching word activity

**Quizzes**
Test your knowledge

**Slideshows**
View images and captions

... and much, much more!

# SPIDERS

# TARANTULAS

## Contents

2  AV2 Book Code
4  The Tremendous Tarantula
6  What Tarantulas Look Like
8  Tarantula Life Cycle
10 Big Bite
12 Scary Hair
14 Home Sweet Home
16 Where They Live
18 Tarantula Safety
20 Create a Spider
22 Test Your Knowledge
23 Key Words/Index

## Introduction

# The Tremendous Tarantula

When people think of a big, hairy, scary-looking spider, they are usually thinking of a tarantula. Tarantulas are some of the biggest spiders in the world.

Many people are afraid of tarantulas. However, others keep them in their homes as pets. These spiders are not as scary as they look.

Tarantulas have eight eyes, but their eyesight is not good. Instead, they use hairs to feel movement around them.

4 Spiders

# What Tarantulas Look Like

Most types of tarantulas are big. Some can be the size of dinner plates. Tarantulas may weigh as much as a package of 32 crayons.

Tarantulas are covered in hairs. These spiders can be many different colors. They have a large **abdomen** and eight hairy legs. Tarantula jaws are different from those of most other spiders. They move forward and down. This helps tarantulas sink their long fangs into **prey**.

There are **996 known types** of tarantulas.

Tarantulas can weigh as much as 6 ounces (170 grams). This is more than **any other spider**.

Tarantulas 7

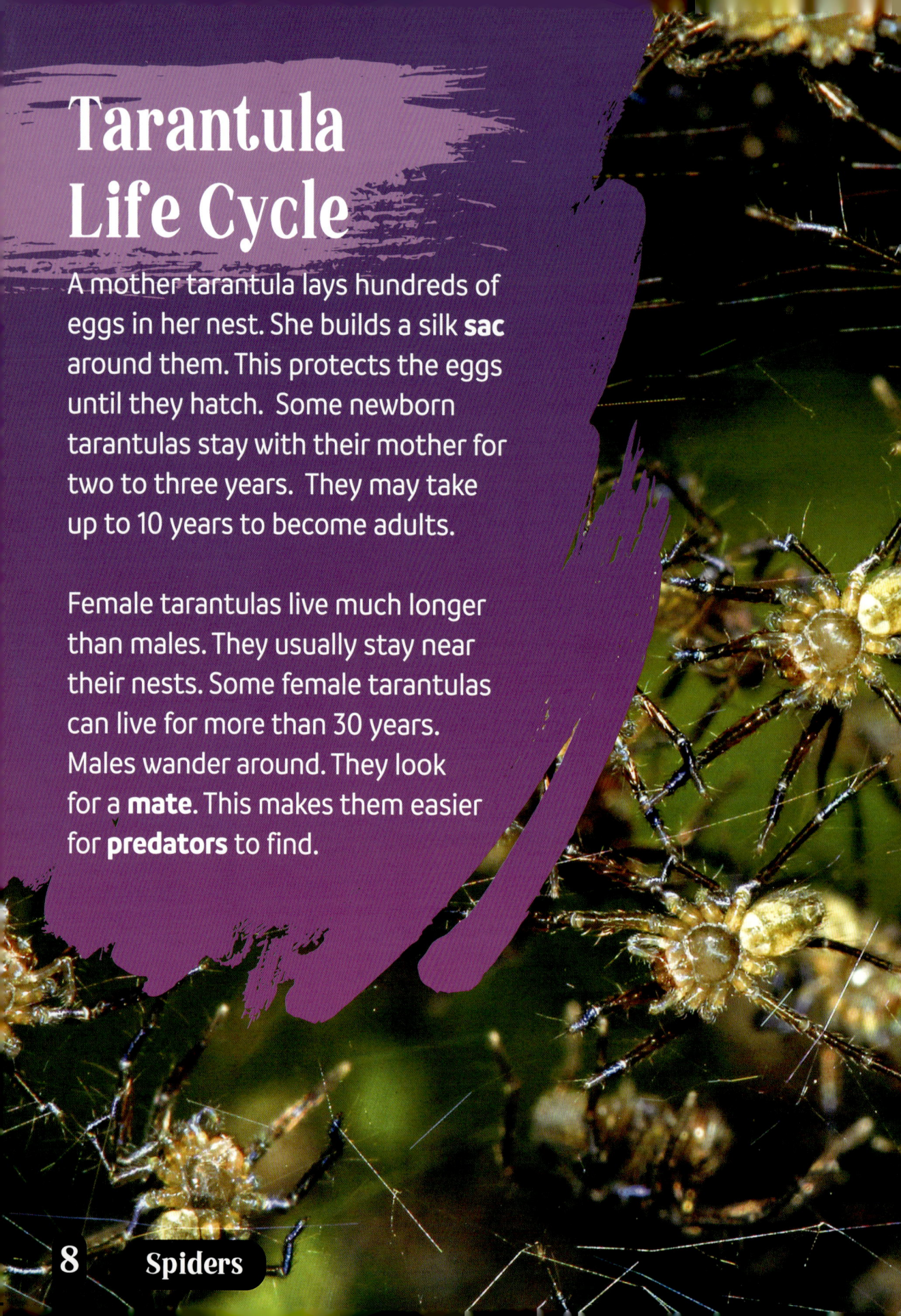

# Tarantula Life Cycle

A mother tarantula lays hundreds of eggs in her nest. She builds a silk **sac** around them. This protects the eggs until they hatch. Some newborn tarantulas stay with their mother for two to three years. They may take up to 10 years to become adults.

Female tarantulas live much longer than males. They usually stay near their nests. Some female tarantulas can live for more than 30 years. Males wander around. They look for a **mate**. This makes them easier for **predators** to find.

# Sizing It Up

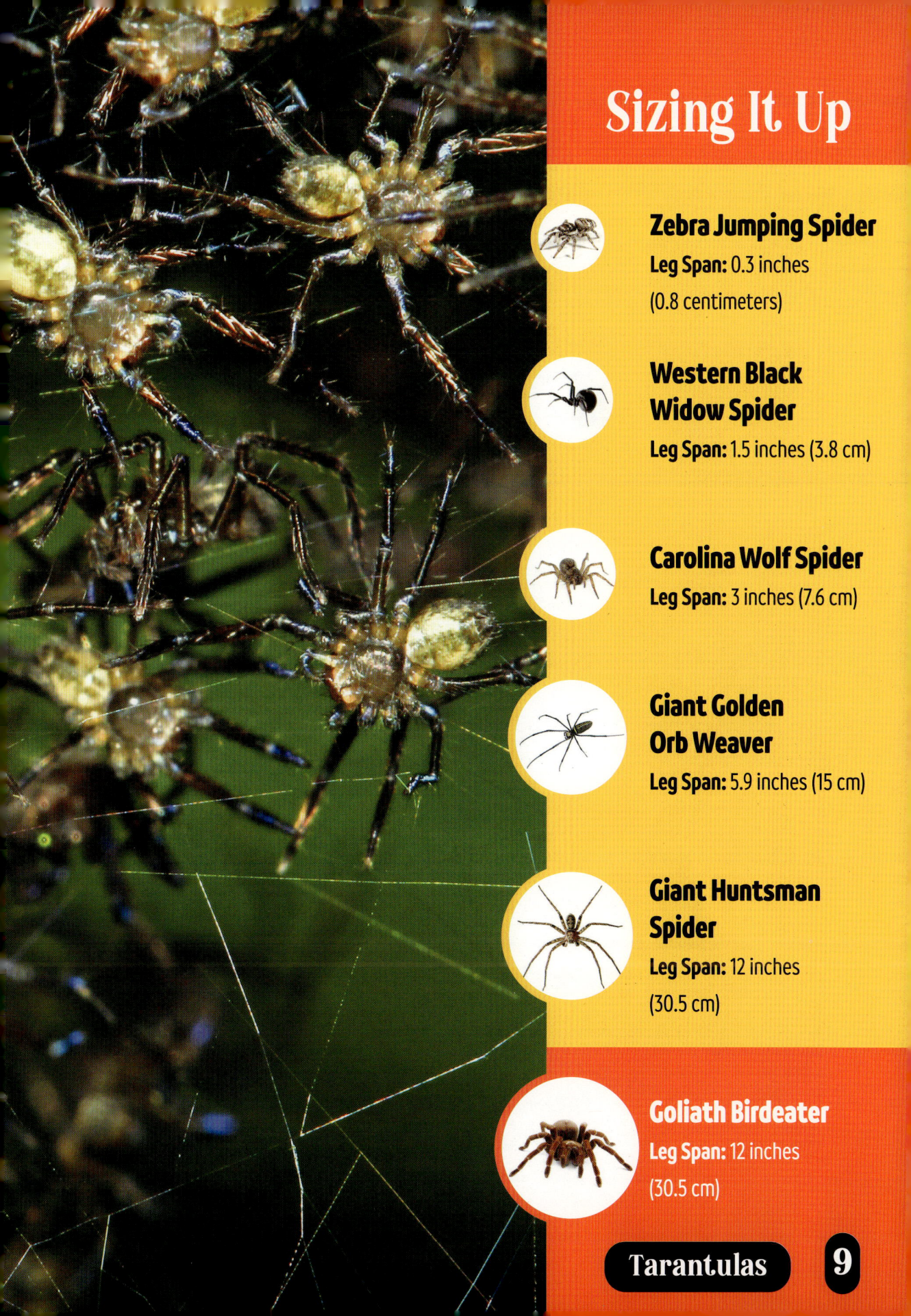

**Zebra Jumping Spider**
**Leg Span:** 0.3 inches (0.8 centimeters)

**Western Black Widow Spider**
**Leg Span:** 1.5 inches (3.8 cm)

**Carolina Wolf Spider**
**Leg Span:** 3 inches (7.6 cm)

**Giant Golden Orb Weaver**
**Leg Span:** 5.9 inches (15 cm)

**Giant Huntsman Spider**
**Leg Span:** 12 inches (30.5 cm)

**Goliath Birdeater**
**Leg Span:** 12 inches (30.5 cm)

Tarantulas

# Big Bite

A tarantula's jaws are specially made for biting. When a tarantula is resting, its fangs are folded under its body. As the spider gets ready to bite, its jaws unfold the fangs. Then, the spider can use them.

A tarantula's fangs are hollow. When a tarantula bites, **venom** moves through them. The venom turns the spider's food into liquid. Then, the tarantula sucks up its meal.

Spot the Fangs!

10 Spiders

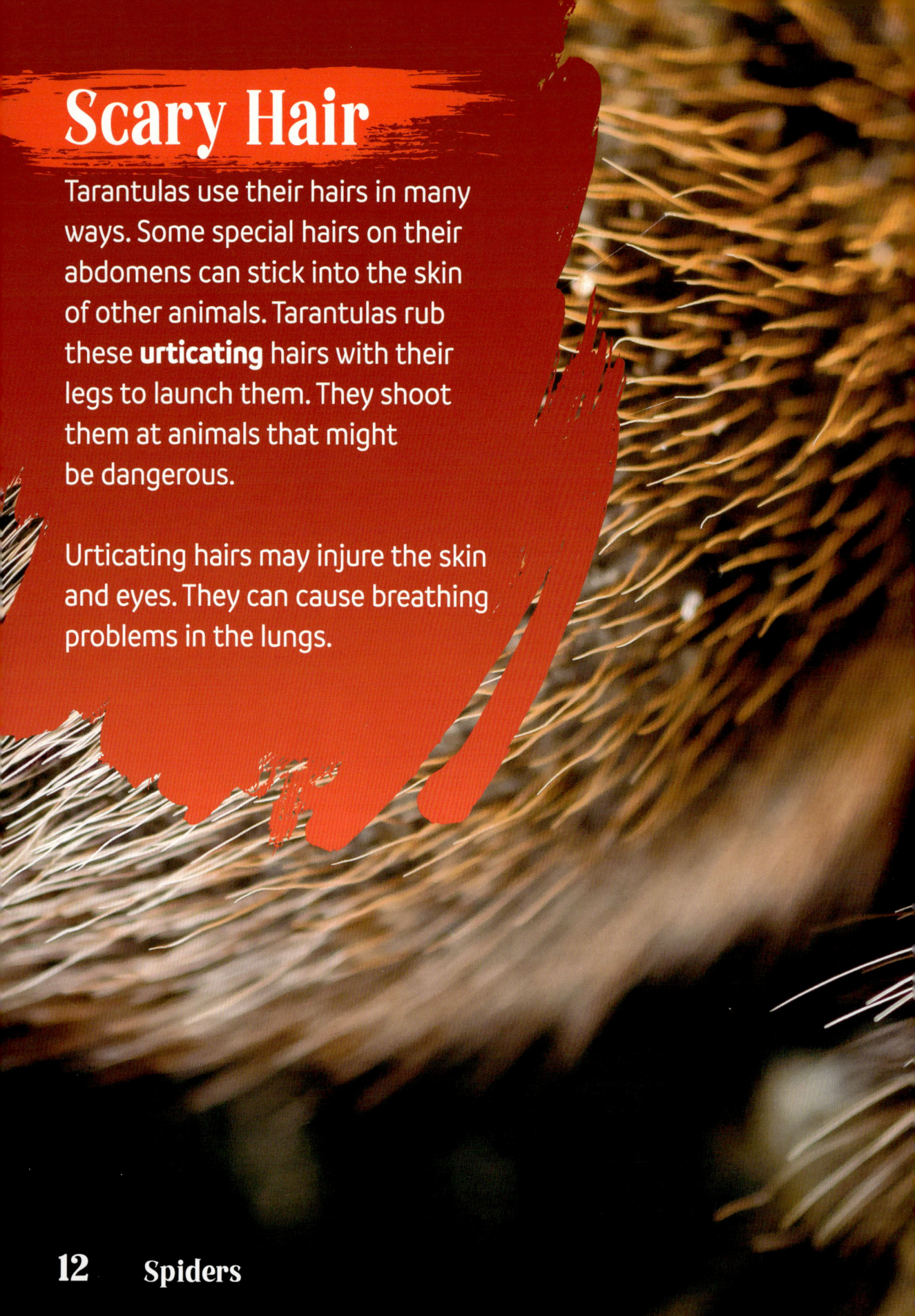

# Scary Hair

Tarantulas use their hairs in many ways. Some special hairs on their abdomens can stick into the skin of other animals. Tarantulas rub these **urticating** hairs with their legs to launch them. They shoot them at animals that might be dangerous.

Urticating hairs may injure the skin and eyes. They can cause breathing problems in the lungs.

Tarantulas 13

# Home Sweet Home

Most tarantulas live in underground **burrows**. They line the walls of their homes with silk. This keeps the dirt from caving in on them. Tarantulas also leave some silk strands in front of their burrows. When prey walks on the strands, the spiders can feel it.

Some tarantulas live in trees. They make tube-shaped nests out of silk.

Most spiders have six pairs of spinnerets for making silk. Tarantulas only have **two pairs**.

Every fall, near La Junta, Colorado, there is a "Tarantula Migration." **Thousands of spiders** leave their burrows to find a mate.

14 Spiders

## Map
# Where They Live

Tarantulas are found in most of the world's warm areas. They are divided into two groups. Old World tarantulas live in Europe, Africa, Asia, and Australia. New World tarantulas are from North and South America.

**Tarantulas around the World**

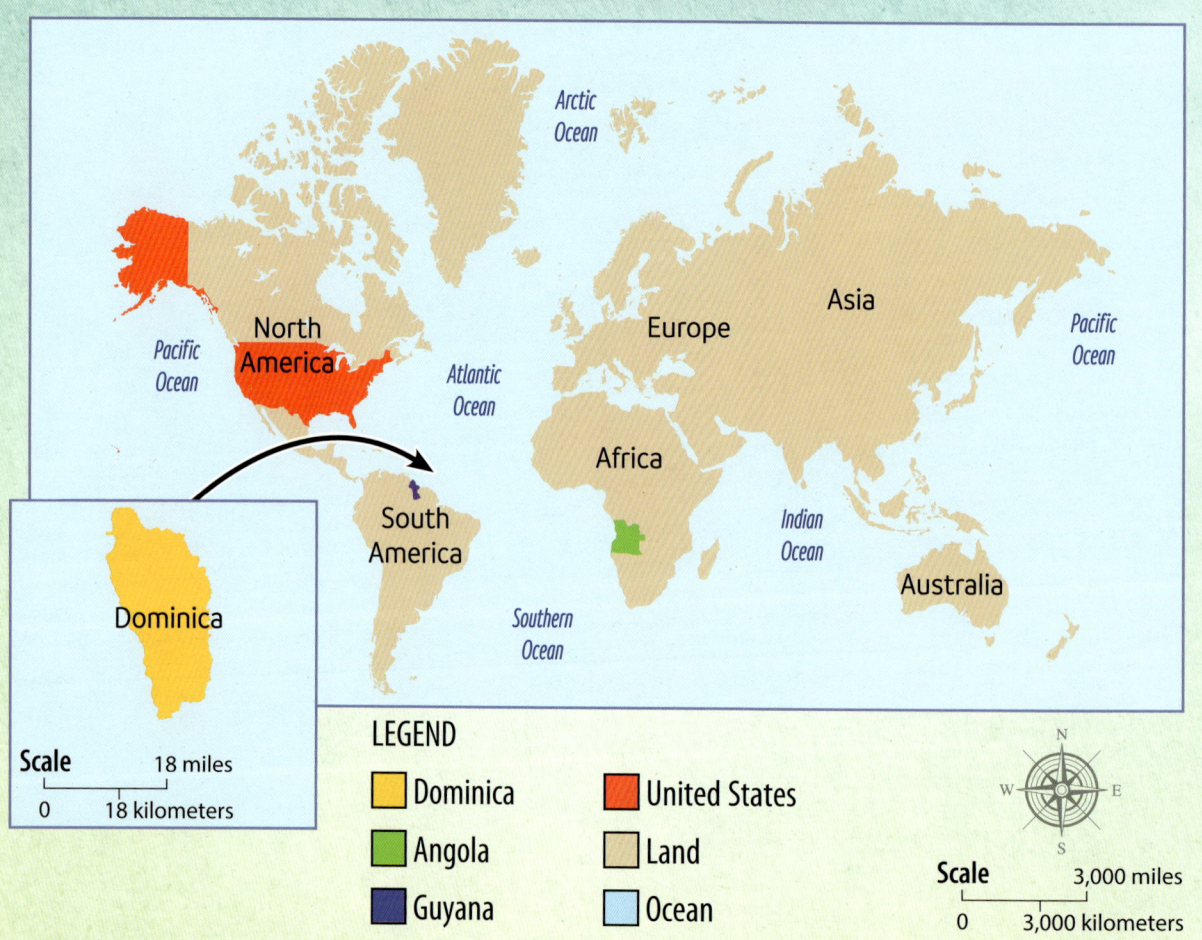

**LEGEND**
- Dominica
- Angola
- Guyana
- United States
- Land
- Ocean

Spiders

### Goliath Birdeater
The goliath birdeater is the largest **species** of spider in the world. Their fangs are about 1 inch (2.5 cm) long. This tarantula lives in South American countries such as Guyana.

Guyana

United States

### Arizona Blond Tarantula
Arizona blond tarantulas live in the southwestern United States. They dig burrows in desert sand. These tarantulas are peaceful and slow-moving. This makes them popular pets.

### Orange Baboon Tarantula
These spiders are also known as "Orange Bitey Things." They have a bright orange color and are known for being **aggressive**. Their bite is very painful to humans. The orange baboon tarantula is found in African countries such as Angola.

Angola

Dominica

### Antilles Pinktoe Tarantula
The Antilles pinktoe is a New World tarantula. It is found in Caribbean countries such as Dominica. These colorful tarantulas live in trees. They can jump as high as 1 foot (30.5 cm).

Tarantulas

# Tarantula Safety

Tarantula owners often wear rubber gloves and goggles when touching their spiders. This protects the skin and eyes.

People should never touch a tarantula in nature. These spiders will bite to protect themselves. Tarantulas do not have strong venom. However, their bites can be very painful.

If a person gets tarantula hairs in their eyes or throat, he or she should go to the hospital. The hairs can cause serious problems in these body parts.

## Activity

# Create a Spider

There are many different kinds of spiders in the world. They all have certain features in common. However, each spider also has its own features. They help the spider live in its home.

**Make your own spider by answering the following questions:**

1. What is your spider called?
2. Where does it live?
3. What features does it share with other spiders?
4. What features help it live in its home? How do these features do this?
5. What does your spider look like?
6. Use pencils, markers, or crayons to draw your spider living in its home. Make sure to include all of its features.

Tarantulas 21

# Quiz
# Test Your Knowledge

**1** How many types of tarantulas are there?

**2** Do female tarantulas live longer than males?

**3** What moves through a tarantula's fangs?

**4** What body part do tarantulas launch into the air to protect themselves?

**5** Do Antilles pinktoe tarantulas live in trees?

**6** What is another name given to the orange baboon tarantula?

**7** Which tarantula is the largest spider?

**8** What should tarantula owners wear when touching their spiders?

ANSWERS: 1. 996  2. Yes  3. Venom  4. Hair  5. Yes  6. "Orange Bitey Thing"  7. Goliath birdeater  8. Rubber gloves and goggles

22 Spiders

# Key Words

**abdomen:** the large back part of a spider that contains many of its organs and silk

**aggressive:** ready to fight or attack

**burrows:** holes dug into the ground that animals use as homes

**mate:** a member of a pair of animals that can reproduce, or have children

**predators:** animals that hunt other animals

**prey:** animals hunted by other animals

**sac:** a pouch or bag that is either part of or made by an animal

**species:** a group of closely related animals or plants

**urticating:** stinging

**venom:** a toxic substance produced by certain animals

# Index

Angola 16, 17
Antilles pinktoe tarantula 17, 22
Arizona blond tarantula 17
burrows 14, 17
Caribbean 17

Dominica 16, 17
fangs 5, 6, 10, 17, 22
goliath birdeater 9, 17, 22
Guyana 16, 17
La Junta, Colorado 14

orange baboon tarantula 17, 22
spinnerets 5, 14
United States 16, 17
urticating hairs 12
venom 10, 18, 22

# Get the best of both worlds.

AV2 bridges the gap between print and digital.

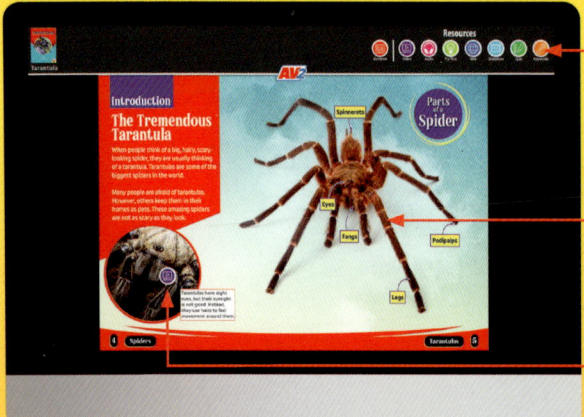

The expandable resources toolbar enables quick access to content including **videos**, **audio**, **activities**, **weblinks**, **slideshows**, **quizzes**, and **key words**.

**Animated videos** make static images come alive.

Resource icons on each page help readers to further **explore key concepts**.

Published by AV2
14 Penn Plaza, 9th Floor  New York, NY 10122
Website: www.av2books.com

Copyright ©2021 AV2
All rights reserved. No part of this publication may be reproduced, stored in a retrieval system, or transmitted in any form or by any means, electronic, mechanical, photocopying, recording, or otherwise, without the prior written permission of the publisher.

Library of Congress Control Number: 2019957414

ISBN 978-1-7911-2296-6 (hardcover)
ISBN 978-1-7911-2297-3 (softcover)
ISBN 978-1-7911-2298-0 (multi-user eBook)
ISBN 978-1-7911-2299-7 (single-user eBook)

Printed in Guangzhou, China
1 2 3 4 5 6 7 8 9 0   24 23 22 21 20

052020
101119

Designer: Terry Paulhus  Project Coordinator: John Willis

Every reasonable effort has been made to trace ownership and to obtain permission to reprint copyright material. The publisher would be pleased to have any errors or omissions brought to its attention so that they may be corrected in subsequent printings.

The publisher acknowledges Alamy, Getty Images, iStock, Minden Pictures, Newscom, and Shutterstock as its primary image suppliers for this title.

View new titles and product videos at www.av2books.com